Unconditional Forgiveness

Lessons on letting go to build better relationships

Sedrik Newbern

Dedication

This book is dedicated to my son. Face every challenge in life with faith and courage. Always know you are destined for greatness because of the generations that have come before you and prayed that your destiny is fulfilled.

Contents

Part II: Healing for Healthy Relationships

Acknowledgements

I want to thank my mom and dad for allowing me to share our story. This process has reminded us all of painful memories. However, we realize the power of forgiveness and the possibilities for healing this book will provide to others. Thank you both for loving me unconditionally and giving me the values and faith in God to succeed in life to become the best husband, dad, and son I can be.

Beside every successful man is an equally successful and supportive wife. I want to thank my wife, Denise Newbern, for unwavering belief in me and encouragement in every endeavor I decide to pursue. Throughout this process and our relationship, you have been my inspiration, my voice of reason, and my confidant as I face challenges head-on with the confidence of knowing you got my back. I love you for loving me so much... unconditionally!

To my editor, Renita Ward, graphic designer, Scott Ventura, of Integraphix, and my wife-photographer, of Precious Gift Photography, thank you all for the time, creativity, patience, support, and honesty you provided in the creation and design of this book.

Introduction

I have wanted for many years to share my perspective on the painful process I went through to build a truly rewarding family life. I am sharing my story to motivate others to move on from past pains and experience unconditional love today.

Despite an early-in-life, troubled relationship with my father and my first marriage ending in divorce, I know it is possible to build better, healthier relationships. After my divorce, I became filled with a great deal of guilt because I had failed at love. I vowed that I would never marry again. As I began to move on with my life and better understand myself, I realized there was an opportunity for a fulfilling relationship even after divorce. Once I forgave myself, I realized my self-worth again and found the happiness in marriage I thought would never be available to me.

The desire to share such life lessons became even stronger and more relevant when I found out my new wife was pregnant, especially when I discovered it was a boy. The fear of repeating the painful cycles from the past made me determined to focus on my marriage and my relationship with my own son. I wrote a lot of my initial thoughts about all this on my blog, unconditionalforgiveness.com. The posts, some of which are compiled in this book, are the manifestation of my life's purpose to help others let go of disappointment.

By no means do I consider myself to be a professional writer or a relationship expert. I do, however, think sharing my past experience as a child of divorced parents can encourage adults today to make better choices as they raise and develop relationships with their children. I also believe having an open dialogue about my disappointment from a previously failed marriage and what others have shared with me in relationship discussions from over the years can offer people a perspective on how to forgive themselves and those who have caused them pain.

It is my prayer that my story and experiences will serve as a guide for others on how to forgive. Through communication and exposure we can all heal and educate others.

Revelations 1:11 – Write in a book everything you see...

Thoughts from My Dad

After leaving my nine-month old son, Sedrik, with his young mom some 40 years ago, I could never have imagined a day like this would ever come.

Deceived by self-centeredness, blinded by foolish ambition, and constantly harassed by a conscience that never slept, I often wondered how a meaningful relationship with Sedrik could ever be possible after I had made such a complete mess of things.

But, thankfully, his mom, her parents and family, and my parents taught him great values, and did not prevent him from having a meaningful relationship with me.

Over the years, several episodes seemed to not be as far from me consciously, as my son was physically.

The first instance was when Sedrik was just a little fellow. On one of my visits to Tennessee, I was so proud to take him an official Mickey Mouse stuffed animal from Disneyland. It actually seemed larger than he was! However, although he seemed very happy to get Mickey, I remember the sad, blank look he gave me when I left.

The next occasion was several years later. I believe he was a "tweener" and came to visit me in L.A. during the summer. It was his little "half" brother's birthday party. Sedrik dressed up as a circus clown and showed that he was obviously an accomplished break-dancer. At least, his little brother thought so! I was amazed how naturally he seemed to embrace his "half" brother and "half" sister and they him. It was as though he was and is their "biological" big brother even still today! However, reality struck when he gently and thoughtfully denied my offer for him to move to L.A. with my new family and go to high school there.

But, I guess the turning point for both of us occurred when Sedrik came to visit me in L.A. when he was about 17 or 18-years-old. He sat down and reflected with me. He had heard a lot about me over the years. This time though, he had come to get to know me for himself. It seems we began this journey then.

Several years ago, Sedrik informed me that he had decided to write poetry. Shortly thereafter, he sent me the most painful poem I have ever read. It was about my many shortcomings during his life as his dad. It described the many times I had not been who he needed me to be, and the many significant milestones in his life I had missed. But, I have never forgot the final phrase, "... but, I forgive you!"

When I read this manuscript, I was amazed at Sedrik's perspective of his childhood. Though painful to read, from my standpoint, it honors his mom, their life together, and how I have been offered a relationship that transcends the cordial and the superficial.

I have come to know Sedrik as a personal friend, a respected husband and father, an accomplished businessman, and the son I always wanted to know! I have been granted what Sedrik calls in this manuscript, "unconditional forgiveness".

I did nothing to warrant this. I have been offered a life I forfeited. I have been given something I could have never earned.

And, I am honored to have been given such an unbelievably undeserved opportunity.

Thoughts from My Mom

I have truly enjoyed reading the blog posts written by my wonderful son. I have learned so much from the writings and feel that I have grown in the area of relationships. It also appears the seeds I have sown, love, caring, integrity and many others have truly yielded a wonderful man. After the separation and divorce from Sedrik's father, my main goal in life was to raise my son to be a good husband – and I must say that he is a loving husband to his wife and an outstanding father to his son.

Growing up in the South in the 1950's and 1960's, there was very little discussion about relationships in my family. My education about relationships actually began in high school from my home economics teacher. When I entered college, needless to say, I learned a lot about relationships. As I mature, relationships have a different meaning in my life. I always share my experience as a single mother and the relationship with my only child, Sedrik. He was encouraged to be open and honest with me and this type of relationship between mother and son is a cherished one.

Where do we begin?

My parents separated when I was only nine-months-old and ultimately divorced, so I spent the first 13 years of my life without a father figure in my house. Thankfully, my mom allowed my dad and me to develop a relationship over the years even though my dad didn't always live up to his obligations.

Once I turned 18, my dad and I had our first man-to-man conversation where I told him that I forgave him for leaving me and that I wanted a real relationship with him. He apologized to me and ultimately forgave himself for not being there for me as I grew up.

We now are best friends and talk regularly about everything. We give each other advice on our marriages, our business ventures, and our favorite sports teams. I can truly say that we have achieved unconditional love and respect for each other in spite of the past.

Don't let your pain be your child's burden

As you can imagine, my mother was really hurt after my father left us. Even after almost 40 years, I still hear stories of how inseparable they were back in college. I know she still cared deeply for him, so how was she able to hide her pain from such a horrific breakup? Why was she so willing to let me spend time with his parents after what their son had done to her young and, dare I say, naïve heart? These are great questions, right?

Unfortunately, I don't have any answers other than she realized I needed a connection to my father. She seemed to believe in her heart my dad was a good man and they just married too young. It may have also been the willingness of W.P., my paternal grandfather, to pick me up and drop me off at my mom's parents' house for summer vacation. W.P. making the 240-mile shuttle run was a big help and he seemed to do it just to spend a few hours with me, his grandson. Again, I don't know the answers, but I'm glad she did what she did... THANKS MOM!!!

My mother rarely let me see the pain she carried over the years due to her failed marriage with my father. This takes a strong woman with character. Even when my dad remarried, my mother always allowed me to go out to Los Angeles to visit him. I have friends (and you know who you are) that will not let their kids go across town to visit their dad and his new family or vice versus. These friends of mine say they don't want their child around the new spouse or significant other. In such a situation, a parent may need to ask inside, "what am I doing to my child by not allowing them to spend time with their other parent?"

As a child, I didn't understand the pain. I only knew that my dad was in L.A., and my mom and I were in Nashville. I knew little to nothing about the challenges they faced in their early 20s living in Washington, D.C., or later, the fights over money. All I knew was that he was my daddy and he lived in L.A., while my mom and I lived in Nashville.

I didn't know what child support was or what financial impact consistent payments could have had on my life. I only knew that my dad was living out in L.A. with the movie stars, Mickey Mouse, and the ocean, and my mom and I were living in Nashville. Fisk University, Tennessee State University, and the music industry were cool, but they failed in comparison to Disneyland, Hollywood, and Santa Monica Beach!

As you can see, a child's perspective is based on things other than parents' feelings. Are you viewing your situation and making decisions through your pain or through your child's eyes? I encourage you to consider the question and have a conversation about your thoughts and/or experiences on this topic both from the perspective of a child and as a parent.

Forgiveness freed my mom from her pain enough for her to allow me to develop a relationship with my dad. Forgiveness of self allowed my dad to be open to having a real relationship with me.

Mom, it's not your fault!

My mom is amazing. Her sacrifices made provisions for my stable foundation, growth, and success. As I reflect on our lives, I am extremely grateful to her! She taught me through her actions what true unconditional love was all about. She set the bar of expectations I would have of any woman who entered my life. **Thank you mom for your faith, strength, and sacrifices!**

With all her greatness, there is one major issue I want to be sure is resolved. It has taken me 40 years to realize that in spite of the man I've become – the loving husband and father I work diligently to be, and the positive relationship I now have with my dad – my mom still feels like she let me down. Are you kidding me?

It's not just my mom. I have encountered several women that somehow blame themselves for a failed relationship and accept full responsibility for challenges with their children that result from an absent father. Why?

A woman doesn't force her spouse to cheat or to be abusive, nor does a woman force a man to neglect his child or children. A woman simply asks a man, a husband to step-up and be the father he vowed to be.

I say to my mom and women everywhere who this applies to – please stop blaming yourself. It's not your fault!

Forgive yourself and forgive him unconditionally so that you can move on. Otherwise, you simply carry the pain with you into the next relationship and you can also pass it along to your children. You hold onto this type of animosity while perhaps your ex has moved on. So in essence you hurt yourself, your kids, and anyone else who is simply trying to love you.

What has been your experience? Have you or your mother not forgiven? Do you or your mother still carry guilt because of an absent

father? Are you finding it hard to forgive and
forget AND move on?

How could it be your fault mom?

From your humble beginnings in west Tennessee
Four brothers, a sister and
one odd job defining your poverty
His 8th grade education,
and her love and guidance
They provided a strong foundation and made you
who you are to me

So how could it be your fault?

You dated my dad
the whole time you were at TSU
They say you two were inseparable,
when they saw Pedro they saw you
It made sense to get married,
and in two years, me you carried
At that time you didn't know
that it'd be just us two

So how could it be your fault?

After I was born, not quite nine-months-old

You were in Washington, D.C.,

lonely with our life on hold

My dad was just too young to raise his own son

So it was up to you to be strong and bold

So how could it be your fault?

You moved us back

to family security in Tennessee

Went back to school

for your master's in child psychology

So I wouldn't be a statistic,

studying fatherless boys fixed it

You loved me, guided me, supported me...

mom you molded me

So how could it be your fault?

You showed me how to make a dollar

out of 15 cents

The sacrifices you made

to provide for me and pay the rent

I never really knew what all you went through
But your investment in my life
was money well spent

So how could it be your fault?

Now that I'm a man and
I've achieved some success in life
I made it through puberty, college,
a divorce, and dealt with strife
I give back to troubled youth all because of you
You taught me how to expect love and support.
Now I share rich, unconditional love with my wife

So how could it be your fault?

You gave me the freedom to explore my last name
You believed in me and
saw what nobody else could see
I've lived my life with respect for you
so that you would never be ashamed
You made me see that I must
treat everyone in a special way

Growing up without a father
didn't matter as much in the end
Thank you for being more than a mom
you've been my very best friend!

Money can't buy love

I still remember the first time I can recall meeting my dad. I guess I was about five-years-old and he brought me a life-size Mickey Mouse from California. I absolutely cherished that Mickey Mouse (almost as much as my Bert and Ernie radio that my grandmother still has at her house to this day). The point is, my dad lived in L.A. with Mickey Mouse and we lived in Nashville. I didn't care that he hadn't sent many birthday or Christmas gifts for the first five years. I just knew that my dad brought me a Mickey Mouse from L.A. and that was the best thing ever! I loved it!

Times were really difficult for my mom financially. I'm sure she talked about the challenges with her friends and family, but she rarely complained about child support to me. As a result, I was able to develop an amazing relationship with my dad in later years based on my own experiences with him. I didn't have to have a grudge because of the failure of my parents' relationship.

We all know that money doesn't buy love. True, you can woo someone with gifts and money, but if there's no substance behind the relationship, IT WILL FAIL. Relationships require commitment and an investment of time to work and become fruitful. I'm just grateful my mother didn't hinge all her decisions regarding my time with my dad on money.

Moms – How many of you have held your child ransom for visitation weekends and holidays over missed child support payments? Do you often speak negatively about your child's father when he doesn't live up to his promises to you and/or your child?

Consider this the next time you want to tell your girlfriends how you really feel about your child's father when your child is present... children are always listening and understand grown-up conversations whether we realize it or not. Hearing such comments could make your child think their dad doesn't want to spend time with them. How hurtful do you think that is for a child? Although you're dealing with your own issues of pain, mistrust, and abandonment, you shouldn't allow such emotions to shape your child's relationships.

Dads – You too can't allow your pain to keep you from your child. Men make excuses to not spend time with their children when the fact is they just don't want to be bothered with their child's mom. Regardless of the issues that exist, remember that your child needs you. They need to see you face your challenges and live up to your responsibilities. Don't wait until you get your money right to get your relationship right with your child! They need your love now!

How many of you men don't want to pay because you think your money is paying for her manicures and shopping sprees. If you were still with her, would you not give her money to do these things anyway? Have you ever considered that maybe; just maybe, she might be able to do these things because she knows that her child's needs are being met with your help? I know this is a tough pill to swallow for many men, but get over it. Remember, that you must take on the responsibility as a man and be a father for your child. If you don't step up, what message are you sending about being accountable for responsibilities? Are you telling your son it is okay to make babies and keep it moving? Are you telling your daughter not to expect to find a responsible man?

And frankly, your responsibilities go beyond that which any court might mandate. Go the extra mile to invest in your child's future with college savings plans and life insurance. Don't wait until their birthday and Christmas to splurge on them. Make every occasion an opportunity to step up beyond child support.

I don't owe you anything

Recently, I was watching an episode of Real Housewives of Atlanta and heard a man say something that made me cringe and want to jump through the TV (though I must admit this show often makes me cringe). Bob Whitfield, an ex-NFL player was confronted by his ex-wife, Sheree Whitfield, about not paying child support in four years. His response was simply that he didn't owe her anything for his kids and that she needs to keep working hard to provide for them. When she threatened to take him to court which would mean guaranteed jail time in Georgia, his response was "do whatcha you gotta do... I'll be waiting for them at my door."

Did he really say that... on TV... on a show watched by 2.9 million viewers? I thought to myself, 'what kind of man are you?' as I watched him. Unfortunately, he said on national TV what many men believe and practice every day.

I understand the challenge that comes when couples separate and are no longer in a relationship with one another. The love is gone. Most times, cupid is replaced with contempt. Anger becomes an easier way to channel the emotions from pain and disappointment. I get it. Rage, hatred even, is definitely a great shield to hide behind. It gives free license to hurt and exact revenge.

To the men who agree with the sentiment of not paying child support, obviously, you don't owe your ex anything. She is no longer your responsibility or obligation.

What about your kids though? Should they be penalized too? Do they need to hurt too because you and their mom cannot be civil and work through your differences? Is this the example of responsibility you want your children to follow? Is this the example of commitment that was set by your parents? Is your love for your children less than your hatred for their mom?

C'mon men! This attitude and behavior reminds me of the kid that gets mad on the playground and takes his ball home so the other kids can't finish the game.

We need to step-up and be men, instead of boys. We need to stop being selfish and start being selfless. We need to stop making excuses and blaming others for our own shortcomings and insecurities. We need to stop and think about the impact of our actions on generations to come.

You owe it to yourself to do everything you can for your children. You owe them your time, your money, your support, your guidance, and most of all your unconditional love and unconditional forgiveness. Don't let their mom or your ego get in the way of you being a dad. Be the absolute best example of a man for your children... better yet for ALL children.

Good fathers impact more than
just their own kids

I used to spend days, if not weeks, at my best friend James "Baby T" Smith's house. He was the first person I met when I started first grade. Eventually, I ended up walking home in the afternoons to hang out at his dad's barbershop on Jefferson Street. I stayed there until my mom got off from work at Meharry Medical College. I know you're asking yourself...an after school program at a barber shop... what mother would allow this? Frankly, in the black community, the barber shop or hair salon is second only to the church. These places serve as hubs for community-building, advice-swapping, comic relief, and unsolicited salespeople. So, my mom was doing what she thought was best for me. Plus, it was FREE!

Before you panic, here's the run down on the afterschool program at JT's Barber Shop. "Baby T" and I got out of school at 3:00 pm. We had just enough time to stop at the store for candy and try to look cool as we walked by the girls' dorms at Fisk University. We had exactly 30 minutes to get to the shop which was just a few blocks away. Once we got there, we had to "get our lessons". JT had to see that we were done before we could go outside to play in the vacant lot across the street or watch the Woody Woodpecker cartoon on TV. And, even before we could go outside or watch our favorite cartoons, we had to restock the drink machine, run to the drug store for JT, and clean up the shop. All the afternoon activities – our homework, odd jobs, and play had to be done before our moms showed up around 5:30 pm.

I learned so much about being a man in those few hours a day on Jefferson Street. There were real men at the shop who talked about real problems, not just about who was going to win the game that weekend. As we got older, we would even engage in conversations with the college guys that were in the shop to get their haircut. I remember many of those guys from Tennessee State, Fisk, and Meharry would always encourage us to get our work done and stay in school.

In addition to the students, JT had a cast of characters that hung out at the barber shop (for those of you that have never had the black barbershop experience, watch scenes from "Coming to America" with Eddie Murphy and Arsenio Hall, and "Barber Shop" with Ice Cube and Cedric the Entertainer, to get a real sense for what I mean by cast of characters).

JT also always had other responsible men around him, many just dropping by to say "hello" and catch up on the latest gossip (yes men gossip too). I watched how JT treated everyone, from Walking Paul, the man who was mentally challenged after coming home from Vietnam and who literally marched up and down the street, to King, the kid that just hung around the shop all the time running random errands. No matter the person, a judge, doctor, handyman or hustler, JT greeted them with a smile and often a joke. He made each person feel welcomed. Most importantly, I saw JT spend quality time with his son. I saw JT teach his son life lessons and be there for Baby T when he needed his dad the most.

Now that I'm a father, I often think back to those moments I observed of my best friend and his relationship with his dad. JT worked hard and sacrificed for his family. Still he somehow always found a way to show up and support those closest to him in whatever they did. JT was also this way with me and so many other kids around the shop and our school. JT helped instill character in me by his actions; He was a great example of being a man and a father. He wasn't my daddy, but I never felt like I wasn't his son.

As my relationship with my dad grew, I realized some similarities between my father and JT. My dad is a giving man, who tries to set a great example for other fathers and children. He loves all of his children and is there for all of us. I'm glad I was able to forgive him unconditionally. The ability to forgive has allowed me to receive the gift of my father's love in a way that I only imagined as a child watching JT and Baby T.

Dads – Are you setting the example for your child and other children around you to show them what it takes to be a REAL man and father? Even if you're not a father, are you sharing your time with children that need a positive male role model?

Moms – Are you surrounding your child with REAL men and fathers? Do you set your own standards high in terms of the type of guys you date and bring around your children?

I hope you can respond affirmatively to these questions. There's a little kid out there – just like I used to be – who needs you to get it right!

I want to be like my daddy

Though I didn't realize it until much later in life, I have always wanted to be like my dad. I seriously thought that my dad was the coolest, soul brother ever and that he could, frankly, do anything... you know like a superhero.

Even though I didn't know much about my dad as a small child, I always wanted to be as cool as I thought he was or as I imagined him to be. He had that 1970's, 1980's swagger that made him "bad to the bone". Everything I experienced in my limited visits with my dad was etched into my brain and magnified by 20 times.

For instance, I've always enjoyed music, even as a young child. Call it genetics, but I remain passionate for good quality music just like the soothing jazz and R&B that my dad played when I was a kid.

I remember my dad taking me to a party at his friend's house in California. My dad walked up to the upright bass in the corner and started plucking away. Well, even now, I have no clue if the notes were right or if it was even a song. All I know is that my dad plucked out some funky tunes on the instrument that epitomizes coolness in jazz... the upright bass.

Let me see if I can make this point even plainer. Once, after watching my dad play the piano in the church basement during one of his visits back home, I knew at that moment I needed to take piano lessons. Unfortunately, I didn't stick with the piano long. A classmate out did me at a talent show and I was done for good, but having seen my dad play made it worth the try.

My dad also sang in a group at church. I can still remember him walking around the house singing, getting his outfit ready on Saturday night. The suits, the shirt, the tie, and the matching pocket square... he was clean! So guess what I did? I sang in school choirs all the way through high school before Glee Club was really cool. I even got to wear a fancy tuxedo with a blue tie and cummerbund when

performing with the Hunters Lane High School
Madrigals. Not quite the swagger I saw with my
dad's musical group, but we were quite snazzy
for a high school chorus.

As you can see, although I didn't grow up
with my dad, I still wanted to be just like him.
He was my biggest role model outside of my
mom and Spiderman. Now, I see my own son
trying to be just like me and I love it!

Unlike Charles Barkley, I embrace the
idea that I am a role model to my son and many
other young men and women. I realize as a man
that I have been and continue to be a role model
to many young people in the absence of their
fathers. This fact inspires me to continuously
give back to my community, set a positive
example for others, and treat everyone with
respect. I know I wouldn't be where I am today if
it weren't for the qualities instilled in me by my
mom, dad, step-dad, aunt and grandparents.

There were other father figures that filled
in the gaps during my dad's absence. The
mentoring by men of Kappa Alpha Psi

Fraternity, Inc., coaches, church leaders, community volunteers, and so many other men that gave me advice helped make a positive impact on my life. These men all showed me what it meant to be a man, father, husband, and son.

Men – Are you making a difference in the lives of young people? Do you give of your time, knowledge, and resources to young men in your community? Have you made the effort to show young women what to expect from a real man so they don't lower their standards? Are you embracing the impact you can have as a role model and mentor for fatherless children?

To forgive, you have to forget

I decided to spend part of my Christmas break with my dad in Los Angeles during freshman year in college. C'mon who wouldn't want to spend a few weeks in 70 degree weather after a tough first semester as a freshman in college? I'd spent summers and Christmas breaks with my dad for the last 10 years, but this trip was going to be different from the other visits. This was the trip to L.A. that would change my life. On this trip, I was 18-years-old, a grown man (or so I thought).

You're probably thinking I was pretty set to have a wild time hanging out in the west coast sun. Fact is, I was quite afraid to leave the house. Dad was living in South Central at the time, about a mile from the heart of Inglewood. This was the late 1980's and gangs ran the block. I was a good-hearted kid from Nashville. I didn't want to get caught in the wrong place at the wrong time. Not to mention, I wouldn't dare wear ANYTHING red or blue.

Funny thing, my dad's favorite outfit was a pair of red sweatpants, blue t-shirt, and red cap. I walked 20 paces behind him when we went out for Mexican on the infamous Crenshaw Boulevard. I figured if a drive-by happened, I wouldn't get shot as long as I looked like I wasn't with him.

Ok, back to the reason this was the moment that changed my life. I had decided that on this trip I wanted to have a heart-to-heart with my dad about our past and our future. I guess that's what you do when you're a grown man right?

It was late in the evening and we were hanging out on the couch when I said to my dad, "For my entire life I've heard how much I'm just like my dad. I've heard a lot of things about you over the years from friends of my mom and family members, and most of it was NOT good."

This statement really got my dad's attention. I continued by saying, "now that I'm grown, I really want to get to know you for myself. I want to develop a real relationship with you as a man. I want you to know that I forgive you for not being there for me growing up. I know you were young and you made mistakes that you wish that you could change. Dad, that's the past and we can't change what happened. So, let's just focus on building our relationship starting today."

That was the moment. In that statement, I had erased 18 years of guilt for my dad and pain for myself.

There went 18 years of regret built up inside of him for not being there for me while I was growing up. There went 18 years of me wondering why. There went 18 years of us both pretending that all of the pain was erased and forgiven.

In that moment, I forgave him and most importantly, he forgave himself. I felt the power of the moment. I could sense the burden of guilt being lifted off my dad. I knew this was a moment that would change my life, but I didn't really know how or to what degree. My dad says to this day he still remembers that moment as a turning point in his life.

We've all heard the sermons in church about unconditional love as it relates to God's love for us. Unconditional love is often mentioned at wedding ceremonies as the guiding principle to a happy, long-lasting marriage. Based on these teachings, I had a pretty good idea what unconditional love meant. I knew that it was a deeper love that remained committed no matter what the circumstances. It meant loving someone in spite of their mistakes and shortcomings.

But one day, I heard a preacher talk about unconditional forgiveness. His message really stuck with me, because I thought, "this means that you have to forgive someone regardless of what they've done to you or a loved one". In other words, you have to forgive AND forget!

I immediately began to think of the families of those that lost loved ones to domestic violence or senseless acts of violence (drive-by shootings, gang violence, vehicular homicide caused by DUI). Sometimes there have been instances of family members extending unconditional forgiveness to the perpetrators.

Now let's be honest. How many of us could truly say that after our little girl or boy had been murdered we could forgive? That kind of forgiveness is rare. It's not easy to forgive when you're deeply wounded, but some people are able to forgive at just those moments.

In my case, I feel that I was able to forgive my dad unconditionally, because I saw in his eyes the pain and regret he felt. I could hear it in his voice when I talked about the things going on in my life. I knew that he was young, immature, and not ready to be a real father to me while I was growing up. How could I truly hold that over his head when I could see the pain he was already in? Once he saw and felt my forgiveness, he was able to open up to me and be a better man, father, and friend. And, I was willing and able to receive and return that openness and build a better relationship with him.

In order to get to unconditional forgiveness, you first have to love yourself and others unconditionally. I challenge each of you, parents and children alike, to seek the power of unconditional love and unconditional forgiveness. Regardless of the pain caused or felt, you should not carry such a heavy burden around with you.

Are you my Daddy?

I've got your brown eyes and your smile
Your personality has been in me
since I was a child

My walk, my talk match you to the book
My height, my build, my hands take a look

When you look at me now,
do you see yourself in me?
Do you see some of your dreams
realized through me?

What makes you see now
what you didn't see then?
Were my brown eyes and smile
not the same in the playpen?

There was so much that you missed in my life
Like my first birthday
and when I first rode a bike

You didn't show me how to shave

or how to tie a tie

Nor did you comfort me

when that girl in high school made me cry

I've accepted that you were young and not ready

So my mom took up the slack

and made my life steady

As I matured into the man that I am

I thanked my mom for teaching

me to be a good man

But there was something missing

that only you could provide

Something that every man needs

deep down inside

I needed your love as only a dad gives his son

To give me the guidance

I've missed since I was one

So I sought that from you and to my surprise

I was an outstanding young man in your eyes

Though I went Kappa you loved me the same
And you made me proud
that I kept your last name
You taught me that
a father's love does not prevent mistakes
And that a father's love
will seek forgiveness no matter what it takes

Now when I need to talk I don't think twice
Because you not only give,
but actually seek my advice

I'm glad to say that I love you
I'm glad to call you my dad
I forgive you...

A father's love helps define a child

Recently we took our son to see Kung Fu Panda 2. In addition to having amazing characters and a storyline, me, my wife, and young son could relate to, there was a very important message in the movie.

There was more than just the typical good vs. evil battle between Po, the main character, and the antagonist in the film, Lord Shen. The colorful animated drama provided lessons I pray my son and many other children will carry with them for life.

As the story unfolded, it is clear that both characters, Po and Lord Shen, had to deal with issues from their childhood that had shaped who they became as adults.

Lord Shen, the evil peacock, had a hardened heart because he couldn't forgive or forget the past. He felt that he had been wronged and decided to take his pain and anger out on the world by destroying Kung Fu.

The one to stop him was Po. He was the panda who had just become the legendary Dragon Warrior. During his quest to warrior-hood, Po discovered Mr. Ping, the noodle shop owner, was not his father. This shocking revelation led Po to set out on an unpredictable journey to find out what happened to his parents and ultimately, who he was.

For sure, Po was confused about his past. In the movie, it was a pretty painful time for him and he could have easily hardened his heart too. His pain could have been an excuse to hurt others. Instead, he accepted who he was and decided to make a difference in the lives of friends and strangers alike.

At the end of his quest, Po went home to Mr. Ping, who was worried that he had lost his son forever. Po proceeded to tell Mr. Ping he knew what happened to his parents. Po concluded the reunion by telling Mr. Ping, "I now know who I am... I'm your son."

Many of us spend our lifetime on a quest to discover who we are. This very natural, human quest is only magnified with the absence of a father in childhood.

Little boys want to know what it means to be a man, a father, and how to treat a woman. Little girls look for a father's love for validation and to set the standard for manhood, marriage, and fatherhood. Even when a child grows up and discovers his or her purpose in life, they still have a strong desire to connect to the past and any missing parts.

Over the years, I have come to know my dad, not as the man that left me when I was only nine-months-old, but as my best friend and confidant. I can truly say that at this point in my life, he is one of the few people that understands me and supports me in all that I try to accomplish.

His unconditional love for me and my development as a man have sustained me during some of my toughest challenges in marriage and in business.

He has also shown me what it takes to be a good father. I watched how he loved and nurtured my brothers and sisters. I've seen how he treats his children by marriage as if they were his own. He's like Dr. Huxtable to his step-children and their friends. He is definitely considered to be one of the coolest dads.

Imagine all that I would have missed if my mom didn't allow my dad to have a relationship with me or if my dad didn't make any attempts to get to know me. Consider the jealousy and resentment I would have had knowing that he was such a great father to my sisters and brothers, if I never had the opportunity to develop a relationship with him myself.

I am so thankful for the relationship I have with my dad and the positive impact he has had on me and my life. Now, as I try to be the best dad I can be for my own son, I am proud to say that I know who I am... I'm my father's son.

Like the gallant cartoon character Po, I've had to do a little searching to be able to know and embrace that fact. Trust me I know life isn't like the movies and there's not always a happy ending. However, I am thankful that if you work hard enough for it – there can be.

I encourage those reading this to seek healing in broken relationships with fathers and cherish those relationships that are already strong!

Son, I want to always be your superhero

Every little boy has a favorite superhero. Whether it's Batman or Spiderman, little boys have an overwhelming desire to be strong and possess the skills to fight the bad guys.

As a kid, I honestly thought I was Spiderman. I wore my Spiderman underoos just about every day. I even had the little web slinging glove (which the 1970's version fails in comparison to what is available today). One Saturday morning after watching Spiderman, I actually went outside with a jump rope that I slung over a tree limb. Somehow, I thought the rope would cling to the tree so that I could swing like Spidey. Of course, it didn't and I landed flat on my back!

Now my son is carrying on the tradition of being Spiderman. He sleeps in Spiderman pajamas every night, wears Spidey socks, and has way too many Spiderman figures, cars, and other gadgets. When I say, "Matthew" he says, "No. I'm Spiderman".

I promise I didn't drill Spiderman into his head. It just came naturally – call it genetics. So far he has not attempted to swing on a tree. Once he does it will make the circle of life complete.

As he continues to grow and develop, it amazes me to watch the similarities we share. I notice that he watches my every move and repeats everything I say (which is not always a good thing). Literally, when I stop suddenly, he bumps right into me. That's because he is usually walking right behind me... in my footsteps.

Growing up without my dad was disappointing and difficult at times, especially since I didn't have siblings to play with. I didn't have a dad to crawl around the house and spray spider webs and attack- the-bad-guy games with me to build up my little ninja skills.

Now that I have my own son, I don't care how crazy I look shooting fake spider webs in public. And yes, I will wear my Spiderman, Batman, and Superman t-shirts with pride. Why? I want my son to enjoy life and explore his imagination. In many ways, I know I'm creating the childhood moments that I missed with my own dad.

Dads – It's easy to get consumed with providing for our families. Work can take over life. We allow deadlines and stress to limit our time spent with our children. Even when we are around, the smartphone is buzzing with emails and phone calls that take our attention away from them. Then we look up and our children are grown and we've totally missed it.

Take time out to spend real quality time with your children. Make sure that you are totally present. It's not easy and frankly in no way am I the perfect example for others! I just pray my son always remembers I was willing to put down my iPad, jump over the couch, crawl under the table, and shoot the bad guys in the other room with my spider webs to keep our house safe.

How do you deal with a life of disappointment?

You don't trust many people. You refuse to let people get close to you. You protect your feelings at all cost, because you know it's just a matter of time before you're disappointed... AGAIN!

Sound familiar? No? Then let's just say that you have a "friend" that fits this description. You notice that your "friend" doesn't invest much energy in their relationships. With family, your friend is happy when they call, but just fine when they don't. In relationships, they never seem to be happy or to trust the person that seems to absolutely adore them. They want to love and be loved, but have erected stone walls around their heart reinforced by steel, electric fencing and even kryptonite. Yes, even Superman can't get through to your heart... I mean your friend's heart.

How does anyone get to such a place?

As children, we are born with absolute unconditional love and forgiveness. Unfortunately, we learn some of our first lessons about disappointment from our parents when they don't keep promises. Broken promises seem to be magnified when two parents are no longer together. Dad promises to spend time at a game, a recital, whatever the occasion, and doesn't show or gets there embarrassingly late. The repeated disappointment doesn't stop the wanting heart from thinking "maybe this time" it will be different. And, each time it's not.

Over the years, there is an expectation deep inside that promises will not be kept. So to protect ourselves, we build up defenses to ensure we'll never be hurt again. As we get older, we seem to pick relationships with people who have commitment issues. Their empty promises to be faithful and trustworthy open the wounds from childhood.

Then we meet our soul mate. We're afraid to open up because so many people we have loved and trusted have disappointed us time after time. So ultimately, our soul mate pays the price for the people that hurt us in the past. Somehow, we justify this emotional baggage because we expect them to eventually hurt us anyway.

Sounds crazy, huh? Well, that merry-go-round is the reality for many people I encounter and frankly has been for generations. So, how does such a cycle break? How can you find and give unconditional love? It begins with unconditional forgiveness.

First, you have to forgive the person or people that hurt you in the past. I realize this is easier said than done. You have to realize you're carrying pain which keeps you attached and weighed down.

Second, forgive yourself. As a child, you were never responsible for any broken promises by a parent. It's not your fault you did not have a picture-perfect childhood. Release the little-kid pain that may be hanging around in your heart. As an adult, forgive yourself for previous or even current hurtful relationships. Ego and pride can make it difficult to accept one's own part in unhealthy relationships. But, face it, now you know better and will do better.

Lastly, you have to be open to the possibilities life has in store for you. Fear keeps us from being vulnerable in relationships and presenting ourselves as we truly are. How can we expect someone to love us unconditionally if we never show who we really are?

Seriously, shed the guilt and just do better. Get over it and move on. Find your happiness!

I don't care enough to let you back in

I've had many conversations with parents and children that struggle with forgiveness since I started exploring this issue more openly. The parents seem to realize their mistakes and have a strong desire to have a relationship with the child they left behind. Ironically, the child doesn't want to have anything to do with them. There's just too much pain and resentment for the child to push aside to rebuild a relationship.

This reminds me of the story in the bible about the prodigal son. If you recall, the young son left the comfort of his home and family to explore the world and all that was good AND bad in it. After realizing the grass was not greener, he decided to go home. His father planned an extravagant homecoming party to celebrate his son's return. The older son was angry because he had stayed at home and did what was expected of him. He couldn't understand why there was a need to celebrate.

The father said his younger son was lost but now had been found again.

I relate people who are struggling with forgiveness to the characters in this story. For example, after a family gets over the pain and shock of a father's abandonment, they create a new life. The family finds a way to manage and get things done. All the while, each family member carries a memory of the father that left. Some long for his return, just as the man in the bible story longed for his son. While others in the family resent the father's departure because of the burden left behind. The brother in the bible story displayed this emotion.

The question is which family member are you going to be when the "prodigal son" returns? Are you prepared to forgive or will you be filled with anger?

The lesson in the bible was all about forgiveness... unconditional forgiveness.

What more must I do to be forgiven?

I was wrong. I knew better. I really didn't consider your feelings, just my own. I'm sorry. I wish I could take it back, but I can't.

How many times have you said these words? When was the last time you admitted that you were wrong? How was it received? Were you forgiven right away or did you have to pay for your mistake for quite a while?

Most of us desire to be forgiven when we have hurt someone that we care about. We will do just about anything to make it right. This is such a challenge for relationships that even the TODAY Show did a segment on "The Art of the Apology".

But what happens when all of your efforts to earn forgiveness are not successful? What do you do if that person is still holding onto something you did days, weeks, months, if not years ago? What if the reason they can't forgive you has nothing to do with you at all? What if the person is not willing to forgive you because what you did reminds them of pain from a previous relationship? How can you win in this situation? Is there anything you can do?

Often we have deep rooted pain that just won't allow us to move on. We think that we're over it, but in fact, we have only suppressed the issues until someone or something reminds us of the situation that hurt us. When we are reminded, the pain sometimes erupts like a volcano of emotion because we never dealt with those feelings and the hurt that occurred in our past. Even when we try to address it, at this point in our lives we can't find the words to articulate the issues or the pain it causes. We just know that it hurts, because it takes us back to a dark place in our past that we vowed to never revisit.

Now, imagine that you are the person that made the mistake and wants to make amends; however, nothing you can do or say changes the way the other person feels. How do you right the wrong? How do you take back what was said? How do you convince them to forgive you and move past this one? Really, how do you push through it?

Saying I'm sorry and admitting fault seems to be the most difficult thing for people to do. Society has shown us (especially our politicians) that even when caught red handed, deny guilt until the very end. So when someone actually admits fault, they have walked out on a very skinny branch. They have admitted they were wrong, imperfect and in essence vulnerable. And then it happens. The denial of forgiveness is for many of us validation that it doesn't pay to open up and admit that you made a mistake.

Ironically, the very person that will not forgive may have already expected the mistake. For them, it wasn't a matter of "if" but "when" we would hurt or disappoint them. In other words, we were guilty until proven innocent. This is a subject for another chapter, but who could ever win in this scenario?

I don't have the answers to this one. I wish I did... trust me! So, maybe the question isn't "what more must I do to be forgiven," maybe the person seeking forgiveness needs to ask the other person "what do you need to do in order to forgive?"

Guilty until proven innocent

When it comes to relationships, have you ever felt like you were serving a life sentence for a misdemeanor that should have only resulted in probation? What do you do? Do you just accept the verdict or do you fight for your innocence?

There are many inmates serving time for crimes they didn't commit. Whether it was a court appointed attorney that didn't serve them well, or the greater judicial system that – because of racial or social economic biases – found them guilty.

I would argue there are definite similarities between the judicial system and relationships... though I know I'm walking on a skinny branch by drawing this parallel and furthering the "ball and chain" idea. That said, I ask that you hear me out on this one.

Often in relationships, you make a mistake and the punishment never seems to fit the crime. No matter what you do, the other person is just not willing to forgive you and move on. You are officially in a "no win" situation... Guilty!

Frankly, many women have told me they expect to be disappointed by guys in relationships. In fact, it's never a matter of "if" but "when". Typically this is the result of pain from previous relationships when a guy disrespected them, didn't live up to the promises made, constantly disappointed them and fell short on their expectations. After being disappointed so often, women simply become jaded and expect the next guy to be no different than the last five guys that hurt them. Because the last guy has moved on and there are still unresolved issues, the next guy to come along unfortunately has to pay the price.

Now to be fair, men have the same issues and frankly misappropriate their pain to unsuspecting and undeserving people in their lives... new women, children, family, co-workers, the kid's soccer coach, the guy at the stoplight, etc.

We all often spend our lives hurting other people because we were hurt and never forgave the person that caused the initial pain. In other words, we never enjoy Agape love (which is selfless, sacrificial, unconditional love and the highest of the four types of love in the Bible) because our hearts are too hardened to forgive others and allow people into our hearts again without conditions. There is power and healing in forgiveness! First, we must forgive ourselves so that we can forgive others.

The wall around your heart

Why do we build walls and fences in our yards? Simply to protect our homes, gardens and flowers from unwanted trespassers like the coyotes and deer that often make tracks through my backyard. We also build walls and fences to keep what's in our yard safe. They provide a safe environment for our children and pets to play. We build walls and fences because we want to keep what's precious and beautiful to us from being harmed, broken, and trampled. Makes sense!

So in essence, the walls and fences we build serve as protection in many ways, or do they? What about the wall you've built around your heart? Is it truly protecting you?

"I'm not going to be naïve ever again. I know this relationship is going to turn out like all the others so why bother investing emotions and time into this one. There's no way I'll ever give my all to another man. I'm tired of being someone else's doormat. I'm going to live for me!"

Ladies, does this sound familiar? We have all felt this way in our lives probably more often than we would like to admit.

For guys, the pain sounds more like, "I poured my heart out in this relationship and she told me that I need to 'man up' and be a real man. I'll never show another woman my true feelings. She will never see my emotions no matter how much I'm hurting. I will never let another woman take advantage of me. I'm going to live for me!"

Do we really turn this pain into motivation to live for ourselves or does the pain become the cross we bear and use to attack others that try to develop a meaningful relationship with us?

We have all invested ourselves in the wrong person. Interestingly, we keep making the same mistakes, but don't realize it until we're too deep. So we end up getting hurt over and over again. Eventually we build walls and fences to protect ourselves.

I would offer that the wall around your heart keeps people from getting in and keeps you from getting out so that you can enjoy the world around you. I encourage you to find a way to forgive yourself and forgive those that hurt you. Whether it was your father, mother, or spouse that left your family, or the boyfriend or girlfriend that walked away with your heart and your pride, you have to keep it moving to live a life of happiness and fulfillment. You have to find unconditional forgiveness!

How Do I Remove the Mask?

How many licks
does it take to get to the center
of your heart – that soft, sweet place
I long to enter?
Just beyond the abyss of hurt,
pain, and broken promises of years past
Is that why you only see the mask?

How can I make a promise to you
that's never before been kept...
When promises were never sincere
why shouldn't you expect
me to fall short of your expectations
when all I want to show you is my appreciation
for the beautiful strong woman you are
and what we have achieved so far?
When all you ever see is the mask!

I look in your eyes
and I see the pain of many years
I see the generational impact

of those lonely and painful tears

You don't blame him

but it was obviously his fault

Why do men cheat when they always get caught!

Now I have to look in your eyes

and all I see is the mask that you see?

Is that really me?

I see through you

what I thought I would never see.

But, I'm a new man now,

because He's truly ordering my path.

I'm in this for better AND for worse,

and this love WILL definitely last.

I'm not who I was, nor am I who I will be,

But put your trust in Him and not in me.

Because of His grace there go I,

and through His grace, I'll love you 'til I die.

But you still don't see me; you see the mask and

think that's where truth hides!

You see the lies told by the past masks to cover

up the emptiness inside.

I've removed my mask so you could truly see me

The kindness and support I'll give

to allow you to be whatever you dream to be.

My life to you is an open book;

it's to you that I run when I need to take a look

behind my own mask to see what's inside

to see the skeletons I continue to hide.

I'm sorry for who I became,

and I'm sorry for all of your shame!

I now know that there's two sides to this pain

but are either of us to blame?

Together we can conquer the world

and change our lives forever,

But we have to remember

that we're in this together.

How do we find what is meant to be

and designed by Him... that is "we",

until eternity

When all you ever see is the mask!

Help me to take it off because it HURTS!!!

After the HOPE is gone

Just a few short years ago, HOPE was the basis for a movement that ignited generations of people with very diverse backgrounds, beliefs, and cultures around one common purpose... change. After decades of disappointment, discrimination, and disenfranchisement, there was a feeling that change was coming to America and the world. There was HOPE for tomorrow.

Where is that HOPE today? Where is all the momentum and excitement? What happens after the HOPE is gone? Can you get it back?

HOPE defined is the feeling that what is wanted can be had or that events will turn out for the best. Without HOPE we go through life with our glass half empty. We never find true happiness because we don't believe we will get nor deserve the best out of life. Hence we can't let go of our past because that is our reality. Moving forward is a challenge since we can't predict our future or guarantee our success. Therefore, any discouraging news makes us cling to our past for safety and ignore our HOPE for a brighter tomorrow.

Imagine you're a trapeze artist. Your entire routine is based on letting go, hoping for the best, and having faith that you can truly move forward without falling. This is no different than how we should live our lives. We can hold on for safety, but we will only swing back and forth through life's ups and downs never moving forward. Or, we can focus on what might happen if we fall, which will again make us squeeze tighter and not let go. HOPE is what allows us to let go, soar through the air, and find there's a new phase of growth and opportunity for our lives.

There are always going to be setbacks and naysayers. So how do you overcome the tendency to cling to the past? You have to let go. The key to letting go is unconditional forgiveness. First, you have to forgive yourself. Then, you have to forgive the person/people that hurt you. Once you have forgiven yourself and others, you can see life without pain... a life full of HOPE and opportunity. That's when you will begin to soar.

You gotta keep it moving

I am often asked, "how do you keep such a positive attitude in the midst of challenges?" I even had a manager once say that I didn't seem engaged because of my calm demeanor and way of approaching challenges. Anyone that truly knows me understands that I am a very passionate and emotional person, but over my life I have learned not to let things out of my control drive me crazy.

Call it what you will, but I realized that I'm too blessed to be stressed. I focus on what I can impact and believe that the outcome will always be in my best interest.

In my business, I have challenged my team to the same mantra which we have coined as POPT – Power of Positive Thinking. With this guiding principle, we are able to focus on the positive outcomes and successes and not dwell on the negative situations and missed opportunities. We simply gotta keep it moving to achieve the goals we have set for ourselves and for our business.

So how do you apply this to your life and relationships? Focus on what you can control. And to paraphrase what the faithful social change agent Gandhi said be the change that you want to see.

My dad and I often talk about the moment that changed our relationship forever. It was the moment that I told him that I forgave him. In this moment, I was the change that I wanted to see in our relationship and he focused on what he could control at that point... forgiving himself.

If you find yourself focusing on negativity and issues from your past, remember this analogy. There's a reason your rearview mirror is small when compared to your windshield.

While you may have heard the analogy before, the point is relevant and worth repeating. Live your life proportionally. Focus on what's ahead of you and only use your past as a reference and to make sure that you have truly moved past the obstacles that once hindered your path. If you focus too much on your past, you will run into another obstacle or miss your next turn toward your big opportunity! This is not just true on an individual level; it is a lesson that applies on so many levels.

In all things, you gotta keep it moving! Focus on what's ahead and not behind you by living a life of unconditional forgiveness.

There's no love without forgiveness

Love is patient and kind. Love is not jealous or boastful or proud or rude. It does not demand its own way. It is not irritable, and it keeps no record of being wronged. It does not rejoice about injustice, but rejoices whenever the truth wins out. Love never gives up, never loses faith, is always hopeful and endures through every circumstance. 1 Corinthians 13:4-7 (NLT)

This is one of my favorite bible verses because it gives us a roadmap on "how" to love without condition. One of life's best examples of how to love is the way a mother loves a child.

I was blessed with an amazing mom and wife. Both of them continue to prove that a mother's love is like none other. Their patience, sacrifice, commitment, and dedication are unparalleled. When I look at my life, there is no doubt my mother loves me unconditionally.

When I look at the bond between my wife and son, I know that she loves him unconditionally.

But what happens when a child disappoints his mother? Does her love fade or is that the time that her love shines through?

Way more often than not, a mother's love allows her to overlook her child's faults and mistakes in life and love them in spite of the disappointment she might feel. This is the definition of unconditional love. But in order to love unconditionally, a mother has to forgive her child and the action that led to the disappointment.

As a child, isn't that the best feeling to hear your mom say, "don't worry about it, I forgive you"? Even as an adult, those seven words still have amazing healing power. There is nothing that hurts me more than to know that I hurt or disappointed my mom, but to have her forgive me always made and still makes me feel better immediately. And, the same is true when it comes to my beautiful wife.

So why can't we love and forgive each other unconditionally as a mother does her child? I assert that it's because we view forgiveness and unconditional love as vulnerability and not for the power that it brings. We feel we just can't expose ourselves for fear of rejection, pain, and abuse. This fear is often driven by the disappointments we have experienced in relationships early in life.

Wounds from disappointment can run deep. However, just as with all wounds, if we do not treat our past wounds they get infected and scab up. The result is a hardness forms in the place of a once tender spot. Though not immediately visible, such an emotional wound is noticeable to others that get close enough. It is also definitely evident when healthy emotional involvement is required for any relationship to grow. The fact is, you know what wounds are in your heart and you know what caused them. Hence you never forget the pain and protect your heart at all costs.

These wounds prevent us from loving unconditionally because we haven't forgiven ourselves and the person that hurt us. So we get stuck and it's hard to move on. We have to understand there is power in forgiveness and that love never gives up, never loses faith, and is always hopeful. It endures through every circumstance. There's just no love without forgiveness.

Give this remedy a try. Examine your past wounds. Apply forgiveness and love generously to the wound. Then, watch closely for the healing that follows.

The Perfect Gift

Early one morning, I climbed out of my cold bed
With visions of a better life filling my head
Why can't I have LOVE that's truly sincere
One that lasts and not based in fear

So I fell to my knees and to God I prayed
That my perfect soul mate would come my way
To love me and accept me with all my flaws
And teach me how to love "just because"

Amazingly, an angel appeared in my life
She coached me on issues
She spoke with honesty and touched my heart
And for her life I prayed for a new start

As our past relationships dissolved
Our support for each other evolved
For her, my attraction began to grow
So I again prayed to God, because I had to know

Is she the Perfect Gift for which I prayed?
That soul mate that I needed to come my way

Or is she in my life just for a short season
To give me hope back... is that the only reason?

After my prayer, I looked deep into her eyes
And that's when He made me realize
This relationship is much deeper than the norm
He is building a foundation to weather any storm

He is teaching us how
to fix things that have been broken
From our hearts and our spirits
to our desire to give a love token
He is giving us a new chance to do things right
He is making us solve problems without a fight

I've learned so much from you about myself
About accepting people for who they
are and not placing them on a shelf

I feel your pain and
I taste your fear of the unknown
I question our issues but
I'm always reminded of how
and why we've grown

You are the Perfect Gift
that I will cherish for life
You are my soul mate,
my Perfect Gift, my wife!

About the Author

Sedrik R. Newbern, president of Newbern Consulting Group, is a highly sought after coach, consultant, author, motivational speaker, and workshop facilitator who specializes in impactful marketing consulting and purpose-driven personal/professional coaching.

A recognized leader in sales and marketing, as well as, career development and relationship coaching, Sedrik has developed and conducted over 300 workshops and motivational keynotes on marketing strategies, sales processes, career development and life transitions for over 1000 individuals over the last 20 years.

Sedrik has also consulted with over 500 small business owners on marketing strategy, processes and measurement. His success as a small business owner and consultant is driven by his ability to develop local value-added advertising and sponsorships with integrated social media and public relations campaigns to create sales opportunities.

Sedrik's seminars, workshops, and consultations are interactive, thought-provoking and life changing. He uses real life examples and hands-on activities, sprinkled with a bit of humor in presentations and sessions to engage participants. This ensures attendees leave with a memorable experience, new ideas, and action plans that are easy to implement.

Sedrik has a deep passion and commitment to grow the community and serve others. He strongly believes that when you know better, you do better. He empowers clients, customers, and other entrepreneurs through education and the development of sustainable action plans.

A native of Nashville, TN, Sedrik holds a Bachelor of Science in Marketing from Western Kentucky University and a Master of Business Administration with a concentration in Economics from Tennessee State University. His ultimate support and motivation comes from his wife, Denise, and their son, Matthew. The family currently resides in the northern suburbs of Chicago, IL.

For more information on this book, or to invite Sedrik to conduct workshops and motivational keynotes, please visit his website: newbernconsultinggroup.com

To stay connected with Sedrik, follow him:

Twitter – @sedriknewbern

Facebook – facebook.com/newbernconsulting

Facebook – facebook.com/sedrik.newbern

LinkedIn – linkedin.com/in/sedriknewbern

Made in the USA
Charleston, SC
13 October 2012